# ✦ *Voices from the Civil War* ✦

# SOUTHERNERS

edited by John Dunn

BLACKBIRCH®
PRESS

THOMSON

✦

GALE™

San Diego • Detroit • New York • San Francisco • Cleveland
New Haven, Conn. • Waterville, Maine • London • Munich

Photo credits: Cover, pages 10, 11, 21, 27 © Library of Congress; pages 10 (Davis), 11 (Lincoln) © Digital Stock;  pages 5, 6, 8, 15, 25, 29 © North Wind Picture Archives; page 13 © Bettmann/CORBIS; page 19 © Hulton Archive; page 23 © Mary Evans Picture Library; page 30 © Scala / Art Resource, NY

**LIBRARY OF CONGRESS CATALOGING-IN-PUBLICATION DATA**

Dunn, John M., 1949-
    Southerners / by John M. Dunn.
        p. cm. — (Voices from the Civil War)
Summary: Provides excerpts from letters, books, newspaper articles, speeches, and diary entries which express various views of Southern Americans toward slavery and the Civil War.
    ISBN 1-56711-794-5 (hardback : alk. paper)
    1. Confederate States of America—History—Juvenile literature. 2. United States—History—Civil War, 1861-1865—Public opinion—Juvenile literature. 3. Public opinion—Confederate States of America—Juvenile literature. 4. Slavery—Southern States—Juvenile literature. [1. Confederate States of America—History—Sources. 2. United States—History—Civil War, 1861-1865—Sources. 3. Public opinion—Confederate States of America. 4. Slavery—Southern States.]
I. Title. II. Series.

E487 .D86 2003
973.7'13—dc21
                                                                                    2002152787

**Printed in United States**
10 9 8 7 6 5 4 3 2 1

# Contents

# THE SOUTHERN WAY OF LIFE

T he American South was a self-sufficient region when the Civil War erupted in 1861. Stretching from Virginia, south to Florida, and westward to Texas, this mostly rural area was dotted with farms that grew rice, tobacco, cotton, and other crops. About 9 million people lived in the South. This number included almost 4 million black slaves. Slaves provided most of the back-breaking labor on large farms called plantations. Southerners had a deep love of their land. They spent much of their time outdoors. They worked on farms, fished, and hunted.

Because the population was spread so thin, most Southerners lived far apart from one another. As a result, they developed a strong tradition of hospitality toward visitors. A code of chivalry, or gracious manners, existed among many members of the South's upper classes. Some members of this wealthy social class often patterned their lifestyles after the nobility of England, their ancestral country.

Most of the South's lower- and middle-class whites were descendants of the Irish, Scottish, and English who settled the area in the eighteenth century. Unlike the North, the South received few of the millions of non-English-speaking Europeans who moved to the United States during the Civil War. As a result, Southerners were more settled in their ways and more resistant to change brought about by immigrants.

Most Southerners, white and black, were very religious. For the most part, they worshiped as Protestant Christians. Few Catholics, Jews, or members of other religions lived in the South.

---

**This woodcut depicts a typical Southern plantation house on the Mississippi River in the 1800s. Plantation owners used African slave labor to produce their crops.**

**Southern slaves busy in their owner's cotton fields are portrayed in this woodcut. Cotton made many a plantation owner very wealthy in the pre–Civil War South.**

Unlike the North, the South was not experiencing great social and economic changes in the years before the Civil War. Nor was industrialization making a great impact on most Southerners. The South, though, prospered from agriculture, especially from growing cotton. Before the war began, many Southern states were among the richest in the country because of the cotton trade.

Most white Southerners were conservative. This meant that the majority wanted to keep social, political, and economic situations the same as they had been for decades. Wealthy whites especially loved their leisurely, agricultural way of life.

Trying to keep a society from changing to meet the times, however, had disadvantages. Many people in the South were poorly educated and knew little of the outside world. Though rich planters and their families were often highly educated, poorer people had little access to books. Few public schools and universities existed in the Old South. Many poor whites could not read or write. Slaves were forbidden by law to learn to read and write.

Nonetheless, many Southerners wanted to preserve their way of life. At the top of Southern society were the plantation owners. Their wealth and social standing gave them great political power. Middle-class merchants, bankers, and small farmers ranked below them. Poor white farmers and laborers came next. At the bottom of the Southern social scale were slaves—black men, women, and children, who were bought, sold, and treated as property.

Slaves had no rights. Some slaves were treated humanely. Others were beaten, tortured, and on rare occasions, even killed by their owners. Though the majority of Southern whites viewed slavery as a natural, God-approved practice, few Southerners actually owned slaves. Only one out of four families owned slaves. Some white Southerners even spoke out bravely against slavery. Still, the majority of whites supported slavery because they considered it to be important to the agricultural economy of the South.

By the 1850s, the slavery issue divided Southerners from their fellow citizens in the North. Most white Southerners resented the growing criticism against slavery. They also were angry that Northern industrialists had managed to persuade Congress to impose taxes on goods imported from other countries. Although this practice ensured that Northern industries would not be undersold, it also raised prices on goods needed by the South.

Different political views also separated the South from the North. Before the Civil War, many white Southerners strongly believed that state governments should have more authority than the federal government. They believed that states had the right to nullify, or cancel, any federal laws they disapproved of. This position, though, put them at odds with most Northerners, who favored the power of the federal government.

These issues and many others persuaded many Southerners that their region had become very different from the North. Northerners also had control of Congress at this time, and Northern interests seemed to be guiding the Union as a whole. By 1860, growing numbers of Southern leaders argued that Southern states should

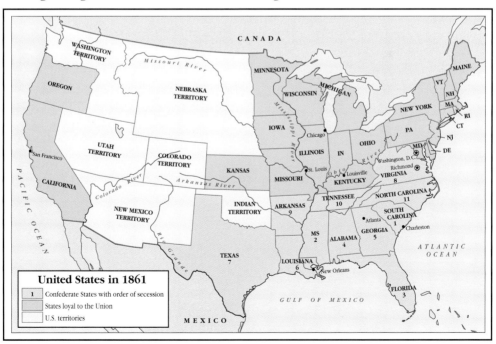

BUILT FROM THE RUINS.

secede, or split away, from the rest of the nation. When Abraham Lincoln, who opposed slavery, was elected president in 1860, whites across the South were angered. They assumed the new president would help pass laws that would end slavery. Fearing this outcome, the state government of South Carolina announced its secession from the Union. It was soon followed by six other Southern states.

In February 1861, secessionist leaders met in Montgomery, Alabama, and created the Confederate States of America. Jefferson Davis became their president. Eventually, the Confederacy included eleven states. Secessionists felt justified in forming this new government. They believed that since the federal government had been created by the states, any state had the right to break away from it when the interests of the state were ignored.

President Lincoln thought otherwise. He believed secession was illegal. He claimed it violated the U.S. Constitution. Confederate troops fired upon federal soldiers stationed at Fort Sumter in the harbor of Charleston, South Carolina, on April 12, 1861. Lincoln responded by instructing U.S. military forces to stop the Southern rebellion. It was the beginning of a civil war that pitted the federal government and the loyal Northern states against the states of the Confederacy.

Southern boys and men volunteered to fight. In many small towns, they formed their own militias. They elected their own officers and drilled and prepared to fight alongside larger military organizations. Women sewed uniforms and flags.

Though slavery was a major cause of the war, most Southern soldiers did not view themselves as fighting to support it. Instead, they believed they were taking up arms to protect both their homeland from invaders and to protect their way of life. Because many Southern males had grown up with guns and horses and were accustomed to living outdoors, they became effective soldiers.

The South gave the Confederacy some of the nation's best military leaders. Time and again, against overwhelming odds, Confederate forces defeated the North. In the long run, though, the armies of a largely rural land proved no match for the power of the industrial North. Four years after the Civil War began, the South found itself divided. Its seaports were cut off from the outside world, and Northern troops burned and destroyed much of its land and many cities. In 1865, the last of the Southern troops surrendered. Not only was the Confederacy destroyed, but so was the Southern way of life. The South lay in ruins. Hundreds of thousands of people were dead or wounded. Slavery existed no more. Blacks and whites in the South, along with their counterparts in the North, were faced with forming a new society together.

**The banner depicted in this woodcut shows the flags of the states that seceded from the Union as building blocks rising as an arch over the broken blocks of the Northern states' flags. The seceded states became the Confederate States of America in 1861.**

# ★ *Chronology of the Civil War* ★

| November 1860 | December 1860–March 1861 | April 1861 |
|---|---|---|

**Abraham Lincoln is elected president of the United States.**

- Concerned about Lincoln's policy against slavery in the West, the South Carolina legislature unanimously votes to secede from the United States. Alabama, Florida, Georgia, Louisiana, Mississippi, and Texas secede from the Union, and form the Confederate States of America.

- Mississippi senator Jefferson Davis becomes president of the Confederacy.

- Arkansas, North Carolina, Tennessee, and Virginia later join the rebellion.

Confederate troops fire on Union-occupied Fort Sumter in South Carolina and force a surrender. This hostile act begins the Civil War.

## September 1862–January 1863

- Lee's Army of Northern Virginia and George McClellan's Army of the Potomac fight the war's bloodiest one-day battle at Antietam, Maryland. Though the battle is a draw, Lee's forces retreat to Virginia.

- Abraham Lincoln issues the Emancipation Proclamation that declares all slaves in Confederate states to be forever free. Three months later it takes effect.

## September 1864

Atlanta, Georgia, surrenders to Union general William T. Sherman, who orders Atlanta evacuated and then burned. Over the coming months, he begins his March to the Sea to Savannah. His troops destroy an estimated $100 million worth of civilian property in an attempt to cut rebel supply lines and reduce morale.

*Jefferson Davis, president of the Confederate States of America*

## July 1861

Confederate troops defeat Union forces at the First Battle of Manassas (First Bull Run) in Fairfax County, Virginia, the first large-scale battle of the war.

## April 1862

• Confederate troops are defeated at the Battle of Shiloh in Tennessee. An estimated 23,750 soldiers are killed, wounded, or missing, more than in all previous American wars combined.

• Slavery is officially abolished in the District of Columbia; the only Union slave states left are Delaware, Kentucky, Maryland, and Missouri.

## June 1862

General Robert E. Lee assumes command of the Conferate Army of Northern Virginia.

*Robert E. Lee*

## August 1862

Confederate troops defeat Union forces at the Second Battle of Manassas (Second Bull Run) in Prince William County, Virginia.

## July 1863

Union forces stop the South's invasion of the North at Gettysburg, Pennsylvania. Lasting three days, it is the bloodiest battle of the war.

## November 1863

President Abraham Lincoln delivers the Gettysburg Address in honor of those who died at the war's bloodiest battle at Gettysburg.

## April 1865

• Confederate general Robert E. Lee surrenders to Union general Ulysses S. Grant. This ends the Civil War on April 9.

• Five days later, President Lincoln is assassinated by actor John Wilkes Booth.

## December 1865

The Thirteenth Amendment becomes law and abolishes slavery in the United States.

*Abraham Lincoln,*
*president of the United States of America*

# ★ George MacDuffie ★
## SLAVERY IS NOT AN EVIL

*Even though most white Southerners never owned slaves, many of them agreed with slaveholders who attempted to justify slavery. A majority of Southerners refused to view slavery as evil as critics in the North and the South suggested. Instead, proslavery Southerners argued that slavery was a natural, time-honored way of life that was good for whites and blacks alike. South Carolina governor George MacDuffie expressed this opinion in a speech he made in 1835. MacDuffie believed God intended for blacks to work as slaves in the South, and that they were not fit for any other kind of life.*

• **George MacDuffie, speech in defense of slavery, 1835.**

**N**o human institution, in my opinion, is more manifestly consistent with the will of God than domestic slavery, and no one of His ordinances is written in more legible characters than that which consigns the African race to this condition, as more conducive to their own happiness, than any other of which they are susceptible. Whether we consult the sacred Scriptures or the lights of nature and reason, we shall find these truths as abundantly apparent as if written with a sunbeam in the heavens. Under both the Jewish and Christian dispensations of our religion, domestic slavery existed with the unequivocal sanction of its prophets, its apostles, and finally its great Author. . . .

That the African Negro is destined by Providence to occupy this condition of servile dependence is not less manifest. It is marked on the face, stamped on the skin, and evinced by the intellectual inferiority and natural improvidence of this race. They have all the qualities that fit them for slaves, and not one of those that would fit them for freemen. They are utterly unqualified, not only for rational freedom but for self-government of any kind. They are, in all respects, physical, moral, and political, inferior . . . . It is utterly astonishing that any enlightened American . . . should suppose it possible to reclaim the African race from their destiny.

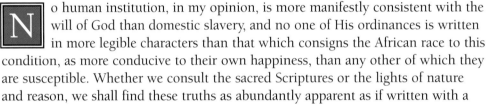

**GLOSSARY**

- **manifestly:** evidently
- **ordinances:** laws
- **legible:** readable
- **consigns:** appoints
- **conducive:** helpful
- **susceptible:** capable of
- **Scriptures:** words of the Bible
- **abundantly:** fully
- **dispensations:** sacred histories
- **unequivocal:** clear
- **Great Author:** God
- **sanction:** approval
- **Providence:** divine guidance
- **servile:** slavish
- **manifest:** evident, obvious
- **evinced:** made clear
- **improvidence:** disregard for providing for the future
- **enlightened:** educated
- **reclaim:** to bring back to a previous way of life

# A Pro-Union Woman of the South
## A QUIET SOUTHERN UNIONIST

*Despite the fact that leaders of their home states voted to secede from the federal government, many white Southerners remained loyal to the Union. Few, however, felt safe publicly criticizing the Confederacy once the war began. Those that did were often yelled at, driven out of town, beaten, or even killed by Confederate sympathizers. The feeling of uneasiness experienced by Southerners who were pro-Union is reflected in the following diary entry of a Southern woman who lived in New Orleans. This entry was written on the eve of Louisiana's secession from the Union.*

- **Harold Elk Straubing, ed., *Civil War Eyewitness Reports.* Hamden, CT: Archon Books, 1985.**

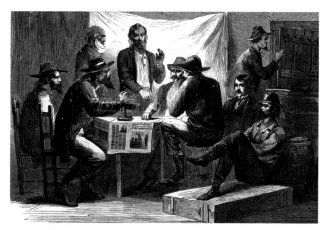

**Some Southerners did not want to leave the Union. Like the men shown here, they had to meet in secret to avoid their pro-Confederate neighbors.**

D ec. 1, 1860. I understand it now. Keeping journals is for those who cannot, or dare not, speak out. So I shall set up a journal, being only a rather lonely young girl in a very small and hated minority. On my return here in November, after a foreign voyage and absence of many months, I found myself behind in knowledge of the political conflict, but heard the dread sounds of disunion and war muttered in threatening tones. Surely no native-born woman loves her country better than I love America. The blood of one of its Revolutionary patriots flows in my veins, and it is the Union for which he pledged his "life, fortune, and sacred honor" that I love, not any divided, or special section of it. So I have been reading attentively and seeking light from the foreigners and natives on all questions at issue. Living from birth in slave countries, both foreign and American, and passing through one slave insurrection in early childhood, the saddest and also the pleasantest features of slavery have been familiar. If the South goes to war for slavery, slavery is doomed in this country. To say so is like opposing one drop to a roaring torrent.

**GLOSSARY**
- **disunion:** a breakup
- **insurrection:** rebellion
- **torrent:** downpour, flood

# ★ John Henry Hammond ★
# A DEFENSE OF SLAVERY

*Fiery speeches about slavery were given across the nation years before the Civil War began in 1861. When Northern criticism of the South's practice of slavery became intense, John Henry Hammond, a wealthy South Carolina slaveholder, decided to respond. In a speech given to the U.S. Senate in 1858, Hammond defended slavery. He used many of the popular arguments of his day. Hammond argued that slavery was a natural part of human society. In addition, he criticized the North for being two-faced on the issue. According to Hammond, critics of slavery did nothing to lessen the misery of poor working whites who worked like slaves in Northern factories. He also suggested most Southern slaves were happy with their situation and lived better than blacks in other countries. These arguments failed to convince many Northerners. Instead, they provoked angry replies and encouraged violence.*

## GLOSSARY

- **menial:** lowly
- **drudgery:** toil
- **constitutes:** makes up
- **mud-sill:** foundation
- **eminently:** highly
- **vigor:** strength
- **docility:** obedience
- **hireling:** someone hired
- **abolished:** done away with
- **compensated:** paid
- **scantily:** poorly, skimpily
- **an elevation:** a step up
- **unaspiring:** without ambition
- **endowment:** abilities
- **galled:** angered
- **degradation:** humiliation

• **John Henry Hammond, a speech in the Senate, 1858.**

In all social systems there must be a class to do the menial duties, to perform the drudgery of life. That is, a class requiring but a low order of intellect and but little skill. . . . Such a class you must have, or you would not have that other class which leads progress, civilization, and refinement. It constitutes the very mud-sill of society and of political government; and you might as well attempt to build a house in the air, as to build either the one or the other, except on this mud-sill. Fortunately for the South, she found a race adapted to that purpose to her hand. A race inferior to her own, but eminently qualified in temper, in vigor, in docility, in capacity to stand the climate, to answer all her purposes. We use them for our purpose, and call them slaves. We found them slaves by the common "consent of mankind," which . . . [is the] highest proof of what is Nature's law. . . . It is everywhere; it is eternal.

The Senator from New York said yesterday that the whole world had abolished slavery. Aye, the name, but not the thing; all the powers of the earth cannot abolish that. God only can do it. . . .

[The North's] whole hireling class of manual laborers and "operatives," as you call them, are essentially slaves. The difference between us is, that our slaves are hired for life and well compensated; there is no starvation, no begging, no want of employment among our people, and not too much employment either. Yours are hired by the day, not cared for, and scantily compensated, which may be proved in the most painful manner, at any hour in any street in any of your large towns. Why, you meet more beggars in one day, in any single street of the city of New York, than you would meet in a lifetime in the whole South. We do not think that whites should be slaves either by law or necessity. Our slaves are black, of another and inferior race. The status in which we have placed them is an elevation. They are elevated from the condition in which God first created them, by being made our slaves. None of that race on the whole face of the globe can

These nineteenth-century factory workers in a Northern city worked hard for little pay. Pro-slavery Southerners argued that their slaves lived better than such free, white laborers.

be compared with the slaves of the South. They are happy, content, unaspiring, and utterly incapable, from intellectual weakness, ever to give us any trouble by their aspirations. Yours are white, or your own race; you are brothers of one blood. They are your equals in natural endowment of intellect, and they feel galled by their degradation.

# ★ *Hinton Helper* ★
# SPEAKING OUT AGAINST SLAVERY

*One of the South's most outspoken critics of slavery was Hinton Helper, a writer from North Carolina. Helper attacked slavery in a book he wrote in 1857. He argued that slavery was morally wrong because it deprived blacks of human rights. He also pointed out that poor white workers were hurt by slavery. Because they competed with slaves who were not paid, poor white farmers and field hands earned very low wages. Thus, in Helper's opinion, slavery damaged the economy for a large section of the South's population. Finally, Helper accused slaveowners of treason if they succeeded in dissolving the Union to keep slavery in place.*

• **Hinton Helper,** *The Impending Crisis of the South: How to Meet It,* **1857.**

W e are unwilling to allow you to swindle the slaves out of all the rights and claims to which, as human beings, they are most sacredly entitled. Not alone for ourself as an individual, but for others also—particularly for five or six millions of Southern non-slaveholding whites, whom . . . [your system] has debarred from almost all the mental and material comforts of life—do we speak, when we say, you *must* emancipate your slaves, and pay each and every one of them at least sixty dollars cash in hand. By doing this, you will be restoring to them their natural rights, and remunerating them at the rate of less than twenty-six cents per annum for the long and cheerless period of their servitude, from the 20th of August, 1620, when, on James River, in Virginia, they became the unhappy slaves of heartless masters. Moreover, by doing this you will be performing but a simple act of justice to the non-slaveholding whites, upon whom the institution of slavery has weighed scarcely less heavily than upon the negroes themselves. You will also be applying a saving balm to your own outraged hearts and consciences, and your children—yourselves in fact—freed from the accursed stain of slavery, will become respectable, useful, and honorable members of society.

And now, Sirs, we have thus laid down our ultimatum. What are you going to do about it? Something dreadful, as a matter of course! Perhaps you will dissolve the Union *again.* Do it, if you dare! Our motto, and we would have you to understand it, is *the abolition of slavery, and the perpetuation of the American Union.* If, by any means, you do succeed in your treasonable attempts to take the South out of the Union to-day, we will bring her back tomorrow—if she goes away with you, she will return without you.

## GLOSSARY

- **swindle:** cheat
- **debarred:** banned
- **emancipate:** free
- **remunerating:** paying
- **per annum:** each year
- **moreover:** in addition
- **balm:** a healing salve
- **ultimatum:** challenge
- **perpetuation:** continuance

# ★ *Sarah Morgan* ★

# UPHOLDING A CODE OF HONOR

*Before the American Civil War, many upper-class Southern whites shared a code of behavior that set them apart from others in the nation. Men and women who lived by this code of chivalry tried to be polite and honorable at all times. During and after the war, though, many of these Southerners allowed anger and hatred to push aside their code of conduct when they were in the company of Northerners, especially Union soldiers. Sarah Morgan, the daughter of a Louisiana judge, lived by the code. In her diary, Morgan recorded her dismay that some Southern women acted rudely toward Northern soldiers who occupied the city of New Orleans in the summer of 1862.*

• **Sarah Morgan,** *The Civil War Diary of Sarah Morgan.* **Athens: University of Georgia Press, 1991.**

Today I believe I am tired of life. I am weary of every thing. I wish I could find some "lodge in some vast wilderness" where I could be in peace and quiet; where I would never hear of war, or rumors of war, of lying, slandering, and all uncharitableness; where I could eat my bread in thanksgiving and trust God alone in all things; a place where I would never hear a woman talk politics or lay down the law. . . . I reserve to myself the privilege of writing my opinions, since I trouble no one with the expression of them; the disgust I have experienced from listening to others, I hope will forever prevent me from becoming a "Patriotic woman." In my opinion, the Southern women, and some few of the men, have disgraced themselves by their rude, ill mannered behavior in many instances. I insist, that if the valor and chivalry of our men cannot save our country, I would rather have it conquered by a brave race, than owe its liberty to the Billingsgate oratory and demonstrations of some of these "ladies." If the women have the upper hand then, as they have now, I would not like to live in a country governed by such tongues.

Do I consider the female who could spit in a gentleman's face merely because he wore United States buttons, as a fit associate for me? Lieut. Biddle assured me he did not pass a street in New Orleans without being most grossly insulted by *ladies*. It was a friend of his into whose face a lady *spit* as he walked quietly by without looking at her. . . . He had the sense to apply to her husband and give him two minutes to apologize or die, and of course he chose the former. Such things are enough to disgust anyone. "Loud" women, what a contempt I have for you! How I despise your vulgarity!

> **GLOSSARY**
> • **lodge:** shelter
> • **slandering:** lying
> • **uncharitableness:** unkindness
> • **valor:** courage
> • **Billingsgate:** pretentious
> • **oratory:** speech
> • **grossly:** glaringly noticeable
> • **vulgarity:** crudeness

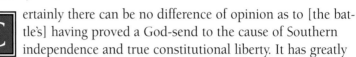

# THE DANGER OF OVERCONFIDENCE

*The First Battle of Bull Run in Manassas, Virginia, took place on July 21, 1861. To the surprise of many, the Confederates won the first major battle of the war. While some Southerners boasted, others were thinking about what lay ahead. A July editorial in the Memphis Appeal, a Tennessee newspaper, warned readers that the worst fighting was yet to come. The editorialist also reminded readers that a desire to punish the South and to make up for its loss at Manassas could motivate the North to plan more successful attacks in the future.*

• *Memphis Appeal*, **July 30, 1861.**

### GLOSSARY

- **impaired:** hurt
- **annihilated:** destroyed
- **subjects:** citizens
- **prestige:** fame
- **like:** similar
- **palpable:** obvious
- **absurdity:** foolishness
- **delusion:** fantasy
- **snare:** trap
- **routed:** beaten
- **stimulated:** excited
- **infamy:** evil
- **evidently:** apparently
- **engagements:** battles
- **magnitude:** size
- **unceremonious:** informal
- **dismissal:** firing
- **incompetents:** incapable officials
- **foreshadow:** suggest beforehand
- **fruitless:** profitless

Certainly there can be no difference of opinion as to [the battle's] having proved a God-send to the cause of Southern independence and true constitutional liberty. It has greatly strengthened the confidence of our people in the ability of their government to maintain itself, even at the point of the bayonet. . . . It has impaired the energies of the "old wreck" of the Federal Government, and has so far annihilated the confidence of its subjects. . . . It has given a *prestige* to the young republic of the South . . . and perhaps . . . [helped the European nations decide whether to recognize the Confederacy as a new nation]. . . .

But to suppose that our independence is an accomplished fact, without other like desperate struggles, is palpable absurdity [that] will prove a delusion and a snare. It is true that the forces of the enemy, outnumbering our own more than two to one, were utterly routed, and driven into a retreat styled by themselves both disgraceful and cowardly. But the defeat is not [going to scare Northern politicians into giving up]. . . . Their pride has been sorely wounded, and their passion of revenge stimulated to the performance of new deeds of infamy. At any sacrifice of life or of the people's money, they will rally their routed forces and attempt with still greater desperation to retrieve their lost fortunes. Relying upon the brute force of mere numbers, the enemy are evidently determined to risk other engagements, perhaps of greater magnitude . . . . The vast preparations that are now being made, and the great caution taken in the efficient organization of the army for the future, with the unceremonious dismissal of incompetents, are but a few of the indications to foreshadow their increased, yet fruitless determination.

# ★ James A. Seddon ★

# CAPTURED BLACK UNION SOLDIERS

Black soldiers played a big role in the Civil War. Though they fought on both sides of the conflict, the vast majority—an estimated 180,000—wore Northern uniforms. The recruitment of blacks caused controversy in both the North and the South. In the North, whites argued that men of African descent would not make good soldiers. Others, however, argued that blacks would fight hard because they were fighting to end slavery. The use of blacks in the U.S. Army particularly upset white Southerners who believed their pres-

**An African American Union regiment storms a rebel fort in this woodcut.**

ence encouraged slave rebellion in the South—an offense for which slaves were punished by death. The following is an excerpt from a November 30, 1862, letter written by Confederate secretary of war James A. Seddon to Confederate general P.G.T. Beauregard. In the letter, Seddon explains the Confederacy's policy of killing captured black soldiers for violating state slave rebellion laws.

• **James A. Seddon, letter to P.G.T. Beauregard, November 30, 1862.**

**S**laves in flagrant rebellion are subject to death by the laws of every slave holding State, and did circumstances admit, without too great delays, and Military inconveniences, might be handed over to the civil tribunals for condemnation. They cannot be recognized in any way as soldiers subject to the rules of war and to trial by Military Courts, yet for example, and to repress any spirit of insubordination, it is deemed essential that slaves in armed insurrection should meet condign punishment, summary execution must therefore be inflicted on those taken . . . under circumstances indicative beyond doubt of actual rebellion. To guard however against the possible abuse of this grave power under the immediate excitement of capture, or through over zeal on the part of subordinate officers, it is deemed judicious that the discretion of deciding and giving the order of execution should be reposed in the General Commanding the Special Locality of the capture.

**GLOSSARY**

- **flagrant:** open
- **tribunals:** courts
- **repress:** restrain
- **insubordination:** disobedience
- **insurrection:** rebellion
- **condign:** deserved
- **summary:** immediate
- **grave:** serious
- **subordinate:** low ranking
- **judicious:** of good judgment
- **discretion:** responsibility
- **reposed in:** placed in the control of

# ★ Mrs. W. W. Lord ★
## SURVIVING THE UNION BOMBARDMENT OF VICKSBURG

*President Abraham Lincoln believed that control of the river town of Vicksburg, Mississippi, was the key to winning the war. He reasoned that by controlling the Mississippi River, the Union could split the South from east and west. Confederate guns on the bluffs of the river near Vicksburg, however, made this task hard to do. After several failed attempts to seize the town, the Union army began a final assault in April 1863. A month later, General Ulysses S. Grant's troops had surrounded Vicksburg. Each day, his men edged closer, while hundreds of Union guns from land forces and gunboats pounded the river town. To escape the constant bombardment, Vicksburg's civilians dug five hundred caves in the clay hills nearby. There they lived—hungry, dirty, and terrified—as the shelling continued for days. Vicksburg resident Mrs. W.W. Lord and her four children were among these cave dwellers. The following selection is from her account of her family's ordeal.*

- **Mrs. W.W. Lord, Journal. Library of Congress Manuscript Division.**

Imagine one of these Vicksburg hills in the very heart of the city—caves underlay even the very heart of it and intersecting each other reaching again to the front, forming in that way several passages and fire openings. In this cave were gathered 8 families besides other single persons . . . .  The firing began to be very steady and severe and the whole hill shook—a large piece of earth fell upon Mrs. McRoas's little daughter and almost killed her . . . .  You can imagine our feelings all shut up in this cave—the horrible shells roaring and bursting all around us and the concussion making our heads feel like they would burst. Poor Mrs. Gunn with her little baby only ten days old!

The next day, Friday, the most terrible battle took place between our batteries and the gunboats,—but we were successful, by the mercy of God, and drove them back. The same day a shell burst at the opening and almost closed it. Mr. Ford and Mr. Merriam were standing almost at the place—such screaming and rushing you never heard. Mr. Merriam exclaimed, "Great God! Out of these caves, out of these caves!" . . .  I have not been undressed now for nearly two weeks and we . . . live on the plainest food. . . .  the children bear

**An old Civil War photo shows the many caves in which Vicksburg, Mississippi, residents took shelter during the 1863 siege by Union forces.**

themselves like little heroes. At night when the balls begin to fly like pigeons over our tent and I call them to run to the caves, they spring up, even to little Louli, like soldiers, slip on their shoes without a word and run up the hill to the cave.

[Mrs. Lord went on to describe the cave the family used for shelter.]

Imagine to yourself in the first place a good sized parapet, about 6 feet high, a path cut through, and then the entrance to the cave—this is secured strong with boards; it is dug the height of a man and about 40 feet under the hill. It communicates with the other cave which is about the same length opening out on the other side of the hill,— this gives us a good circulation of air. . . . I have a little closet dug for provisions, and niches for flowers, lights and books—inside just by the little walk is our eating table with an arbor over it and back of that our fireplace and kitchen with table [etc.]. In the valley beneath is our tent and back of it the tents of the generals. This is quite picturesque and attractive to look at but Oh! how wearisome to live.

# ★ *A Girl from Virginia* ★
# A ROMANTIC VIEW OF WAR

*During the Civil War, many Southerners reacted to the conflict with horror, sadness, and regret. Others experienced feelings of outrage, anger, and revenge. Some, though, were spellbound by the adventure promised by war. In the following excerpt of a diary entry, a young Virginia girl reveals her fondness for the famous Confederate war heroes and dashing young officers in uniform she met while the soldiers marched toward the Battle of Gettysburg in 1863. She expresses special admiration for the way her own loved one appeared in the parade of troops.*

- **Harold Elk Straubing, *Civil War Eyewitness Reports*. Hamden, CT: Archon Books, 1985.**

T hat was a day to remember! [Confederate general Robert E.] Lee's whole army was in Culpeper. Pennsylvania and Gettysburg were before it, and the army was making ready for invasion. On a knoll where a Confederate flag was planted and surrounded by his staff sat General Lee on horseback; before him, with a rebel yell, dashed [J.E.B.] Stuart and his eight thousand cavalry. There was a sham battle. Charging and countercharging went on, rebels yelled and artillery thundered. Every time the cannons were fired we would pile out of our carriage, and as soon as the cannonading ceased we would pile back again. General Stuart happened to ride up once just as we were getting out.

"Why don't you ladies sit still and enjoy the fun?" he asked in amazement.

"We are afraid the horses might take fright and run away," we answered.

I shall never forget his ringing laugh. Our lean and spiritless steeds had too little life in them to run for anything—they hardly pricked up their ears when the guns went off.

How well I remember Stuart as he looked that day! He wore a fine new uniform, brilliant with gold lace, buff gauntlets reaching to his elbows, and a canary-colored silk sash with tassled ends. His hat, a soft, broad brimmed felt, was caught up at the side with a gold star and carried a sweeping plume, his high, patent-leather cavalry boots were trimmed with gold. He wore spurs of solid gold, the gift of some Maryland ladies—he was very proud of those spurs—and his horse was coal black and glossy as silk. And how

## 📖 GLOSSARY

- **knoll:** small round hill
- **sham:** mock
- **cannonading:** heavy firing of artillery
- **steeds:** horses
- **buff:** light brown
- **gauntlets:** protective gloves
- **sash:** waistband
- **plume:** feather
- **resplendent:** splendid
- **sustain:** maintain
- **command:** military unit
- **field lasses:** binoculars

**Confederate general J.E.B. Stuart (right) was known for his daring raids against Union forces as well as for his stylish appearance.**

happy he was—how full of faith in the Confederacy and himself!

My own cavalry officer was there, resplendent in his new uniform—I had it made up for him in Richmond. Dan was very proud of the way I got that uniform. . . . He told General Stuart its history, and that is how a greatness not always easy to sustain had been thrust upon me. General Stuart thought me very brave—or said he thought so. The maneuvers of Dan's command were on such a distant part of the field that I could not see him well with the naked eye, and General Stuart lent me his field glasses.

# ★ *Phoebe Yates Pember* ★
# WORKING IN A WAR HOSPITAL

*Hospitals during the Civil War were commonly overcrowded, understaffed, and lacked medicine and other supplies. Phoebe Yates Pember, a superintendent of a wing of the Chimborazo Hospital, in Richmond, Virginia, left this description of the difficulty she experienced working in the hospital. As Pember notes, amputations were common treatments for many types of wounds. Unfortunately, the loss of a limb invited infection and typically ended in the patient's death.*

- **Phoebe Yates Pember,** *A Southern Woman's Story.* **New York: G.W. Carleton, 1879.**

## GLOSSARY

- **apprehended:** perceived
- **vital:** life-giving
- **commence:** begin
- **yearning:** longing
- **furlough:** vacation
- **wearisome:** tiring
- **advisability:** practical advantage
- **prompt:** immediate
- **invariably:** always
- **enfeeble:** weaken
- **stalwart:** sturdy
- **indifference:** uninterested attitude
- **inflammation:** swelling from an infection
- **mingling:** mixing
- **pyaemia:** a blood disorder
- **officiating:** on duty, acting

The duty which of all others pressed most heavily upon me and which I never did perform voluntarily was that of telling a man he could not live, when he was perhaps unconscious that there was any danger apprehended from his wound. The idea of death so seldom occurs when disease and suffering have not wasted the frame and destroyed the vital energies, that there is but little opening or encouragement to commence such a subject unless the patient suspects the result ever so slightly. In many cases too, the yearning for life was so strong that to destroy the hope was beyond human power. Life was for him a furlough, family and friends once more around him; a future was all he wanted, and he considered it cheaply purchased if only for a month by the endurance of any wound, however painful or wearisome.

There were long discussions among those responsible during the war, as to the advisability of the frequent amputations on the field, and often when a hearty, fine-looking man in the prime of life would be brought in minus an arm or leg, I would feel as if it might have been saved, but experience taught me the wisdom of prompt measures. Poor food and great exposure had thinned the blood and broken down the system so entirely that secondary amputations performed in the hospital almost invariably resulted in death, after the second year of the war. The blood lost on the battlefield when the wound was first received would enfeeble the already impaired system and render it incapable of further endurance.

Once we received a strong, stalwart soldier from Alabama, and after five days,—nursing, finding the inflammation from the

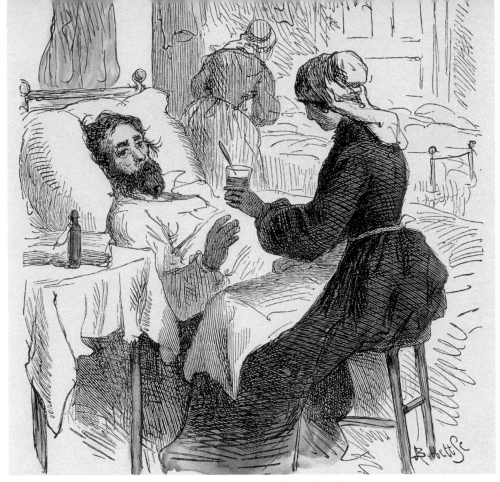

**American women played a greater part in the Civil War than in any other American war. Most volunteered as nurses, as depicted in this drawing.**

wound in his arm too great to save the limb, the attending surgeon requested me to feed him on the best I could command; by that means to try and give him strength to undergo amputation. Irritability of stomach as well as indifference to food always accompanying gun-shot wounds, it was necessary, while the fever continued, to give him as much nourishment . . . as possible. . . . Every precaution was taken, . . . and the arm taken off by the most skillful surgeon we had. After the amputation, which he bore bravely, he looked as bright and well as before, and so on for five days—then the usual results followed. The system proved not strong enough to throw out the "pus" or inflammation; and this, mingling with the blood, produced that most fatal of all diseases, pyaemia, from which no one ever recovers.

He was only one of numerous cases, so that my heart beat twice as rapidly as ordinarily whenever there were any arrangements progressing for amputation, after any length of time had elapsed since the wound, or any effort made to save the limb. The only cases under my observation that survived were two Irishmen.

# ★ *City Leaders of Atlanta* ★
## PLEA TO SPARE ATLANTA

*In May 1864, President Abraham Lincoln had doubts about the Union army's ability to defeat the South. "I am going to be beaten and unless some great change takes place, badly beaten," he said. Lincoln hoped, however, that an ongoing military campaign, led by General William Tecumseh Sherman, might provide the "great change" he so badly needed. As part of a massive effort to cripple the South's ability to wage war, Sherman led ninety-eight thousand men from Chattanooga, Tennessee, into Georgia. Sherman's army wrecked and burned everything along their march to Atlanta. Despite heavy fighting, Union forces controlled the city by September 1. On September 11, Sherman received the following letter from Atlanta's city leaders that conveyed their plea to him to spare their city from destruction. The general, however, was unmoved by the letter. He gave residents time to leave the city and then ordered his men to burn Atlanta.*

- **Letter from the City Leaders of Atlanta to General Sherman, September 11, 1864.**

**S**ir: We the undersigned, Mayor and two of the Council for the city of Atlanta, for the time being the only legal organ of the people of the said city, to express their wants and wishes, ask leave most earnestly but respectfully to petition you to reconsider the order requiring them to leave Atlanta.

At first view, it struck us that the measure would involve extraordinary hardship and loss, but since we have seen the practical execution of it so far as it has progressed, and the individual condition of the people, and heard their statements as to the inconveniences, loss, and suffering attending it, we are satisfied that the amount of it will involve in the aggregate consequences appalling and heart-rending.

Many poor women are in advanced state of pregnancy, others now having young children, and whose husbands for the greater part are either in the army, prisoners, or dead. Some say: "I have such a one sick at my house; who will wait on them when I am gone?" Others say: "What are we to do? We have no house to go to, and no means to buy, build, or rent any; no parents, relatives, or friends, to go to." . . .

We only refer to a few facts, to try to illustrate in part how this measure will operate in practice. As you advanced, the people north of this fell back; and before your arrival here, a large portion of the people had retired south, so that the country south of this is

**GLOSSARY**

- **organ:** voice
- **petition:** ask
- **attending:** that goes with
- **in the aggregate:** as a whole
- **heart-rending:** sad
- **accommodate:** make room for
- **subsistence:** food
- **feeble:** weak
- **subsist:** live

**A small part of the devastation of Atlanta by Union general William T. Sherman's army is shown in this photo. Despite pleas from city leaders, Sherman burned the great city to the ground in 1864.**

already crowded, and without houses enough to accommodate the people, and we are informed that many are now staying in churches and other out-buildings.

This being so, how is it possible for the people still here (mostly women and children) to find any shelter? And how can they live through the winter in the woods—no shelter or subsistence, in the midst of strangers who know them not, and without the power to assist them much, if they were willing to do so?

This is but a feeble picture of the consequences of this measure. You know the woe, the horrors, and the suffering, cannot be described by words; imagination can only conceive of it, and we ask you to take these things into consideration.

We know your mind and time are constantly occupied with the duties of your command . . . but thought it might be that you had not considered this subject . . . and that on more reflection you . . . would not make . . . helpless people be driven from their homes, to wander strangers and outcasts, and exiles, and to subsist on charity? . . .

In conclusion, we most earnestly and solemnly petition you to reconsider this order, or modify it, and suffer this unfortunate people to remain at home, and enjoy what little means they have.

# ★ Mary Elizabeth Dickison ★
# HONORING THE SOUTH

*Despite losing the war and seeing their way of life destroyed, many white Southerners chose to remain loyal to the values of the South. In an 1890 book on the role Florida played in the Civil War, Mary Elizabeth Dickison wrote a tribute to the Southern cause. In the following passage from her book, Dickison expressed the attitudes of many fellow Southerners who were heartsick about the South's defeat and the notion that the Southern way of life would be changed forever.*

• **Mary Elizabeth Dickison,** *A Memoir of the War in Florida.* **1890.**

I am daily reminded of a grievous error that is creeping into the minds of our young people, and it is one that those who lived in ante-bellum days must unite in trying to root out. It is a word—the "new" South—coined from alien brain, and should be blotted from our vocabulary.

A new era in the history of the domestic relations existing between master and servant—the establishment of a new form of servitude—no more indicates a "new South," than the dismantling of a dear old homestead of its ancient furniture and refurnishing with that of modern style makes that dear sanctuary a new home. Let us never give such misnomer to our dear Southland. For us there is no "new South." . . .

The death-knell of the cause we so bravely defended did not destroy the vital powers of our dear Southland, nor was she buried beneath her bloodstained battle-fields, or the desolation of her ruined cities and once prosperous homes. Impoverished as she was, despoiled of her wealth, her productive rice lands and fertile cotton-fields laid waste by one stroke of a despot's pen, she has nobly come forth conqueror in the battle for life.

With that mastery of mind that has ever characterized our people in every noble work and great enterprise, they have built up the waste places, restored order where all was disorder and misrule, and, with indomitable will, called up their hidden forces from the "vast

## 📓 GLOSSARY

- **grievous:** upsetting
- **ante-bellum:** prewar
- **coined from alien brain:** created by outsiders
- **servitude:** slavery
- **dismantling:** taking down and removing
- **sanctuary:** sacred place
- **misnomer:** wrong name
- **death-knell:** the tolling of a bell at a funeral
- **vital:** life-giving
- **impoverished:** poverty-stricken
- **despoiled:** robbed
- **fertile:** very productive
- **despot:** tyrant
- **indomitable:** unconquerable
- **inexhaustible:** abundant
- **gypsum, phosphate and lime-rock:** three common minerals
- **transcendent:** supreme
- **Washington:** George Washington
- **sires:** fathers

**As the Civil War ended, this Southern couple, still attended by their black servant, mourned with many other Southerners the loss of loved ones and their way of life.**

deep"—the grand resources that our magnificent old Southland offers in her rich mines, long hid in the mountain regions, and her inexhaustible beds of gypsum, phosphate and lime-rock found in her lowlands.

With untiring energy are they toiling to make for the rising generation a future of such rich promise as will grandly illustrate the spirit of the old South—true to her heritage of brain and transcendent moral courage. We can never forget our time-honored customs, or the traditions of our people—their generous, whole-souled hospitality, and the courtly dignity that marked the native-born Southern gentleman. Such memories are the "sweet chimes that sound through the haunted chambers of the heart like some old poet's rhymes."

The great roll of illustrious names, from Washington down to our own day, will have added luster, when other names are enrolled—those of our noble rising young men—if they will but prove worthy sons of their noble sires, and keep sacred the honor and fair fame of our dear old Southland.

# ★ *Edward A. Pollard* ★

# THE FALL OF RICHMOND

**Richmond, Virginia, burns, signaling the end of the Civil War.**

*By 1865, a series of Union victories convinced many Northern leaders that it was just a matter of time until the South fell. Union forces had divided the South, controlled major Southern seaports, devastated Georgia, and repelled a massive Southern attempt to invade the North. Then on April 2, 1865, General Ulysses S. Grant, commander of the Union forces, delivered a deathly blow to the Southern cause. His forces captured Richmond, Virginia, the capital of the Confederacy. To avoid capture, Southern troops, along with most leading government officials, including Confederate president Jefferson Davis, fled the city. In the following selection, Edward A. Pollard, a reporter for a local newspaper, the* Richmond Examiner, *provided a firsthand account of the panic, confusion, and destruction of that day.*

## GLOSSARY

- **impending:** upcoming
- **unassailed:** undisturbed
- **unvexed:** untroubled
- **wrapt:** wrapped
- **infernal:** hellish
- **conflagration:** fiery destruction
- **baleful:** threatening
- **plunderers:** robbers and destroyers
- **plunder:** loot
- **satellites:** aides, staff

- **"Evacuation and Fall of Richmond," by Horace Greeley and Edward A. Pollard, 1865.**

M en, women, and children rushed from the churches, passing from lip to lip news of the impending fall of Richmond. And yet, it was difficult to believe it. To look up to the calm, beautiful sky of that spring day, unassailed by one single noise of battle, to watch the streets, unvexed by artillery or troops, stretching away into the quiet, hazy atmosphere, and believe that the capital of the Confederacy, so peaceful, so apparently secure, was in a few hours to be the prey of the enemy, and to be wrapt in the infernal horrors of a conflagration! . . .

"Morning broke upon a scene such as those who witnessed it can never forget. The roar of an immense conflagration sounded in their ears; tongues of flame leapt from street to street; and in this baleful glare were to be seen, as of demons, the figures of busy plunderers, moving, pushing, rioting, through the black smoke and into the open street, bearing away every conceivable sort of plunder."

# FOR FURTHER READING

## Books

Stephen Currie, *Life of a Slave on a Southern Plantation*. San Diego: Lucent Books, 2000. Filled with period illustrations and extended quotations from Southern blacks and whites, this book gives the reader a vivid look at the world of the Southern plantation before the Civil War.

Ann Graham Gaines, *The Confederacy and the Civil War in American History*. Berkeley Heights, NJ: Enslow, 2000. An informative book that explains the beginning of the Confederacy, life in the towns and countryside of the South, and many other aspects of the Confederate government.

Corrine J. Naden and Rose Blue, *Why Fight? The Causes of the American Civil War*. Austin, TX: Raintree Steck-Vaughn, 2000. This book analyzes the complex causes that led to the Civil War.

James P. Reger, *Life in the South During the Civil War*. San Diego: Lucent Books, 1997. Filled with excerpts from primary sources, this book covers many of the social and economic conditions during and after the war.

Virginia Schomp, *The Civil War*. New York: Benchmark Books, 2002. This book contains excerpts of letters, diaries, and personal reflections written by women, children, merchants, slaves, and others whose lives were affected by the Civil War.

Christy Steele with Anne Todd, *A Confederate Girl: The Diary of Carrie Berry*. Mankato, MN: Capstone Press, 2000. An illustrated book that features the six-month diary of a Georgia girl who was loyal to the Confederacy. Most of her diary focuses on the battles fought near or around Atlanta.

## Websites

**The American Civil War Home Page**
http://sunsite.utk.edu/civil-war  The largest online directory of Civil War resources, maintained by Dr. George H. Hoemann of the University of Tennessee. Includes biographical information on Confederate generals.

**The Civil War Home Page**
http://www.civil-war.net  A database of Civil War history, with detailed information on specific battles and campaigns.

# INDEX